BOYS LIKE ME

Jesse Sullivan

Copyright ® 2023 Big Dreams Kids Books

All rights reserved. Published by Big Dreams Kids Books, an imprint of Rascal Face Media and Rascal Face Press.

No part of this book may be reproduced or transmitted in any form or by any means, electronic or mechanical, including photocopying, recording, or by any information storage and retrieval system without written permission from the publisher.

Printed in the USA.

Contents

1   Lin-Manuel Miranda 8

2   The Wright Brothers 17

3   Rajah Caruth 24

4   Guy Fieri 29

5   José Hernández 37

6   Jimmy Donaldson....................... 42

7   George Washington Carver 49

8   Matt Turner 56

9   Neil deGrasse Tyson..................... 62

10 Henry Ford 67

11 Jackie Robinson 74

Contents

12 Steve Irwin **81**

13 Alfred Nobel **87**

14 Dwayne Johnson **94**

Dear Reader,

A super amazing kid like you needs some awesome role models. You need role models who are brave and persistent. It's important to have heroes to look up to. These people might inspire you. They might teach you about working hard and not giving up.

The stories you are about to read are amazing true stories about famous people. I know what you might be thinking. What do I have in common with a famous person? There is no way that I can relate to a famous person. These people may seem important or special, but they were once a kid, just like you!

These boys played games and had cool hobbies. They learned new things and tried new things. Sometimes they were good at them and sometimes they failed. These famous people sometimes felt scared and nervous. They had to be brave and face their fears just like you do.

Have you ever tried something new and not been very good? Have you ever felt like you were a little different from everyone else? Have you ever known the right thing to do, but it still felt scary? All the boys in the stories you are about to read have felt exactly like you! Even though these men made history, they were once boys who had the same feelings you do.

I'm going to let you in on a secret. You have everything you need to make history, too. It's what's inside you. It's what makes you brave. It's what makes you know when to do the right thing (even when it's scary). It's what makes you a good helper and a kind person. I'll bet you're the kind of kid who will make history, too.

When you read these spectacular stories of boys who

made history, remember that they were kids just like you. See if you can picture yourself in their stories. I'll bet you'll be able to relate to them better than you think. After all, they were once a kid just like you.

1

Lin-Manuel Miranda

The young boy tapped his feet. *Tap, tap, tappity-tap!* The music of Broadway show tunes filled the room. He turned the music louder. He loved the loud trumpet and the way the singers sang in harmony.

On the bus the next morning, the driver cranked up the music. The bus bounced along to a hip-hop beat. The lyrics flew

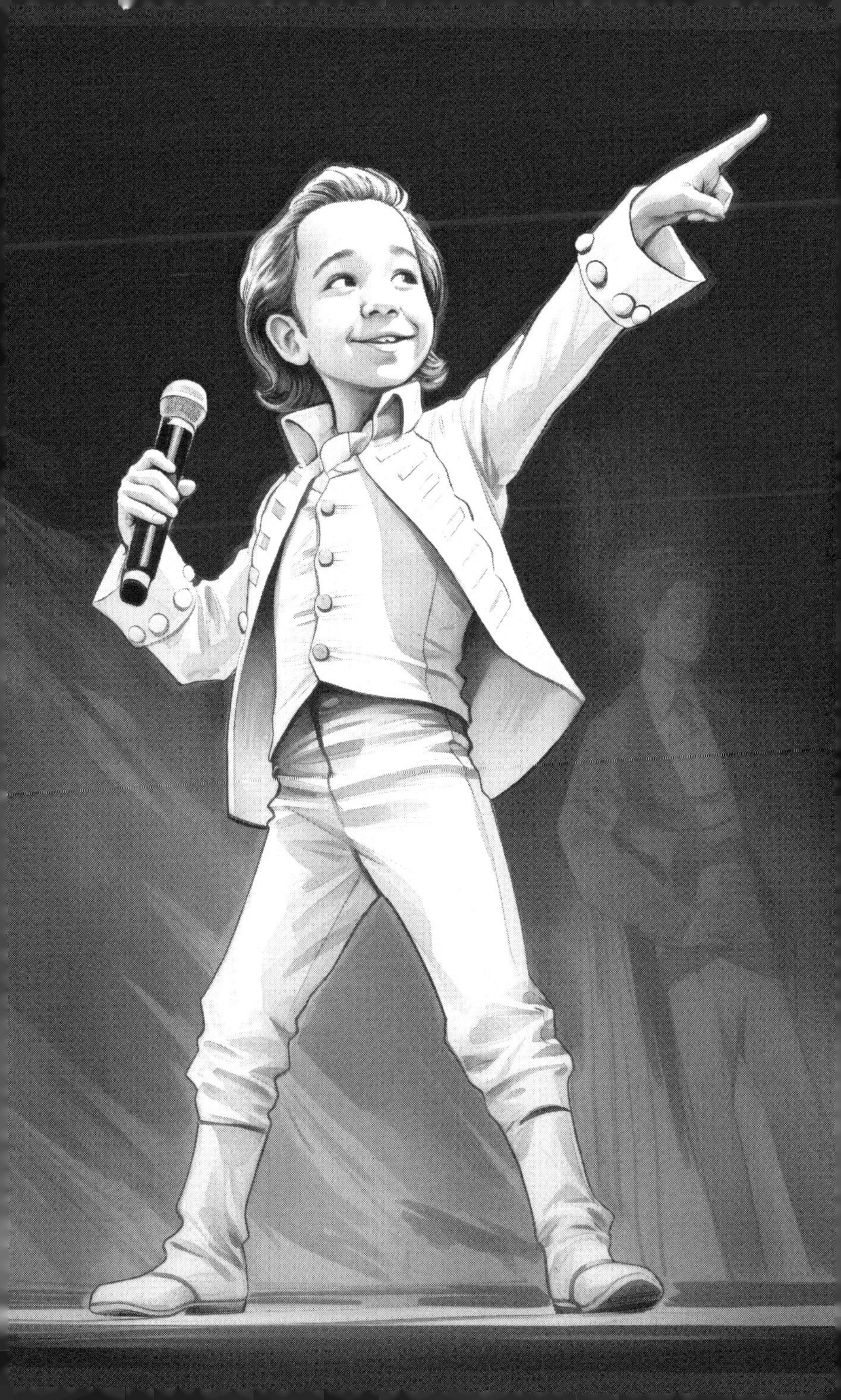

fast and loud. The boy loved the way the song told a story.

The boy listened to the music of the city as he grew up in New York. Funky beats mixed with show tunes. The music of different people and cultures mixed together in his head, and he loved all of it.

Lin-Manuel Miranda grew up loving all types of music. There was just something about the way it made him feel. It woke him up inside. It excited him! He loved when a song could tell a story.

Lin-Manuel listened to his father and mother sing show tunes. His bus driver taught him all about rap and hip-hop. He listened to music from other countries and found beats that he liked. He memorized songs so he could sing along full blast. He didn't know what he wanted to do when he grew up, but he knew that music would be a part of it.

When he was 7 years old, Lin-Manuel performed in his first piano recital. He was excited but nervous. He played his song carefully. The audience clapped. This made him proud.

"I know another song!" he said.

He played another song. Each time the audience clapped, Lin-

Manuel would come up with another song to perform. He loved hearing the people clap and cheer for him. After the fourth song, the teacher made him let another piano student have their turn. It didn't matter though. Lin-Manuel had found another thing he enjoyed. He loved performing!

Lin-Manuel started acting in plays and musicals at his school. A musical is a play with lots of songs. Lin-Manuel liked to sing and dance. Most of all, he loved to write plays and songs. He started writing short plays and musicals. He and his friends would perform them for students and teachers. Lin-Manuel was good at it. He could make the audience feel a certain way with each play and song.

In college, Lin-Manuel wrote his first big musical, *In The Heights*. He also starred as the main character. The play was a big hit! It went on to be a Broadway show, and Lin-Manuel won some big awards. He was just getting started.

A few years later, Lin-Manuel read a book while on vacation. The story inspired him.

"That would make a great musical," he thought. So he got to work.

It took several years, but finally, it was ready. The musical *Hamilton* was a huge success! Lin-Manuel combined hip-hop and show tunes to tell a story that was fast and fun. Everyone loved it. Lin-Manuel also starred in *Hamilton* when it first came out. People thought he was so clever for the new way he was telling a story. This wasn't the boring old theater that people usually thought about. Lin-Manuel made it fun and exciting!

Lin-Manuel really loved to tell stories through his songs. He started working with Disney. Here he could write songs for the characters in movies. It was so much fun to bring these characters to life with their songs! Lin-Manuel wrote the songs for many movies you have probably seen. He wrote the songs for *Moana*, *Encanto*, and *Mary Poppins Returns*.

When he was a boy, Lin-Manuel just knew he loved music. He didn't have a favorite kind. He loved all music. He let all the music around him inspire him. He turned something he loved into his life's work. How cool is it to love something and get to do it every day? What is something that you love to do? What inspires you? With hard work and passion, you can do anything!

2

The Wright Brothers

Do you have a brother or a sister? Do you play together and have fun? It can be fun to have a brother or sister who is always ready to play and explore.

Wilbur and Orville Wright were two brothers who did everything together. They are best known as the Wright brothers. Thanks to them, people can now fly in airplanes!

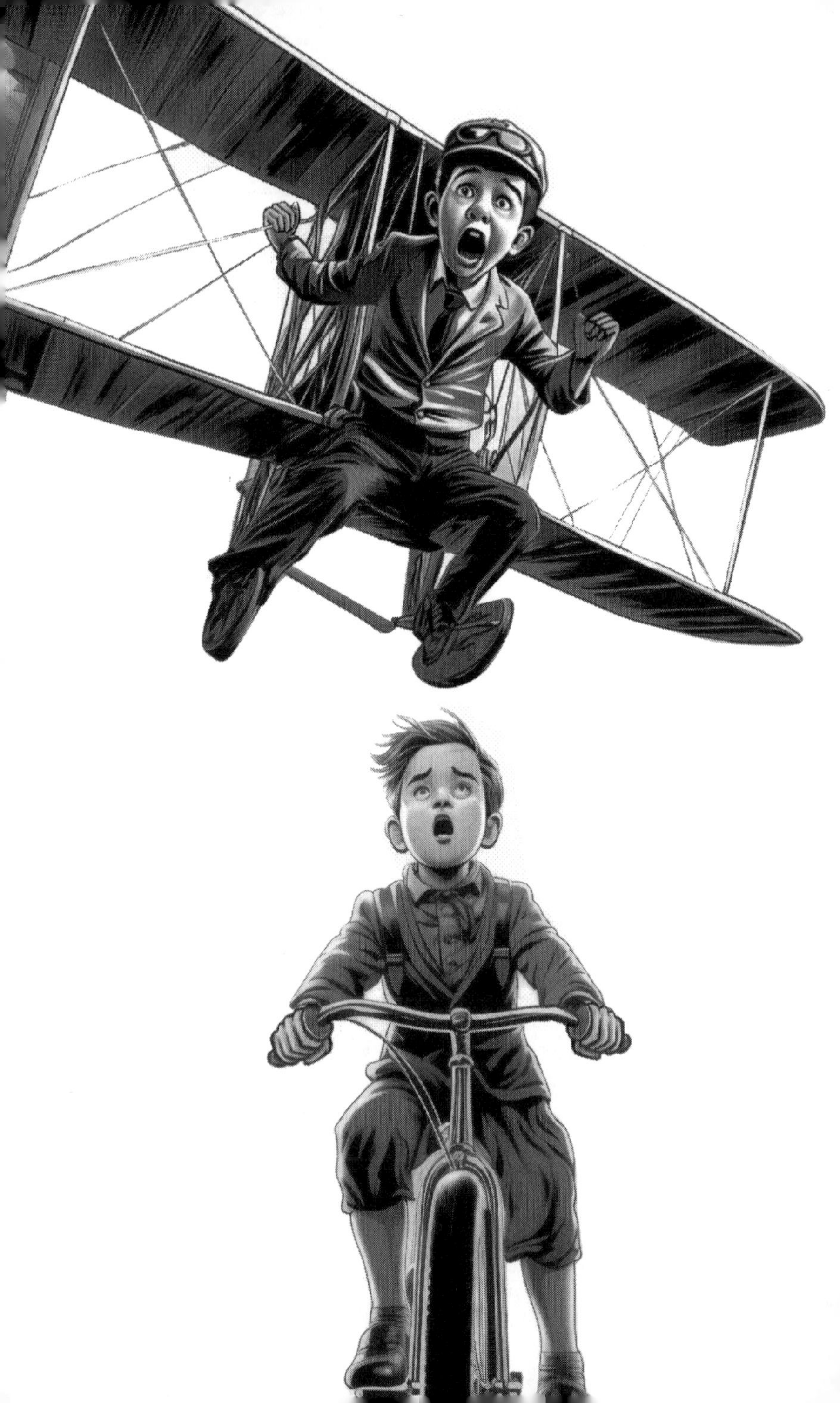

The Wright Brothers

When Wilbur and Orville were growing up, their family moved many times. Wilbur and Orville were brothers, but they were also best friends. They did everything together. Orville and Wilbur shared all their toys. They each had things they were good at doing. This made for a good partnership.

Wilbur loved to read and write. He was very smart. He read nearly all the books in his father's library. Wow! That's a lot of reading. Wilbur liked to write, too. He made his own printing press. He and Orville even printed a weekly newspaper for their town.

Orville liked science. He liked learning how things worked. Orville would often take the toys apart and put them back together. This way he could understand how the toys worked. Orville was a bit of a rascal. He usually got into more mischief than Wilbur. Do you think you are more like Wilbur or Orville?

One day, their father brought them home a cool new toy. It was like a little helicopter and it could really fly. It had a rubber band that turned the propeller. The propeller made the toy fly. The boys loved it! It was their favorite toy. They played with it until it broke and then they built their own. They decided right then that one day they would find a way to build something big so that they could fly!

Wilbur and Orville always worked together, too. For many years the boys worked together and printed newspapers. When they got tired of that, they opened a bicycle shop. The Wright brothers were good at building bicycles, but they still wanted to learn more about flying.

It is good to be curious. The Wright brothers wanted to fly, but how? They started tinkering.

It wasn't easy. They tried many ideas. Finally, they had the best chance yet. The Wright Flyer was their best aircraft. It had a wooden propeller, cloth wings, and a small engine. They took it to the beach. Would it fly?

The first airplane launched into the air. It soared 120 feet. That was all they needed! The Wright brothers knew it could be done. Their teamwork paid off!

For years, the brothers kept working together. They knew that they worked best together. Teamwork makes the dream work! They built many other airplanes and flew many miles.

The brothers only flew together in the same airplane one time. Why? They made a promise to their dad. He was always worried the plane would crash. This made him feel better.

The Wright brothers show us that we all have special things that we are good at doing. When we work together with others, we can achieve amazing things. It is awesome to be curious and use your special gifts to learn new skills.

3

Rajah Caruth

Rajah Caruth proves that with a little bit of bravery and a lot of hard work, you can achieve all your biggest dreams.

Rajah grew up in the city. He saw the movie *Cars* when he was a kid and he was captivated! He loved watching the cartoon cars race around the track. He loved thinking about driving those cars and going fast. Rajah began

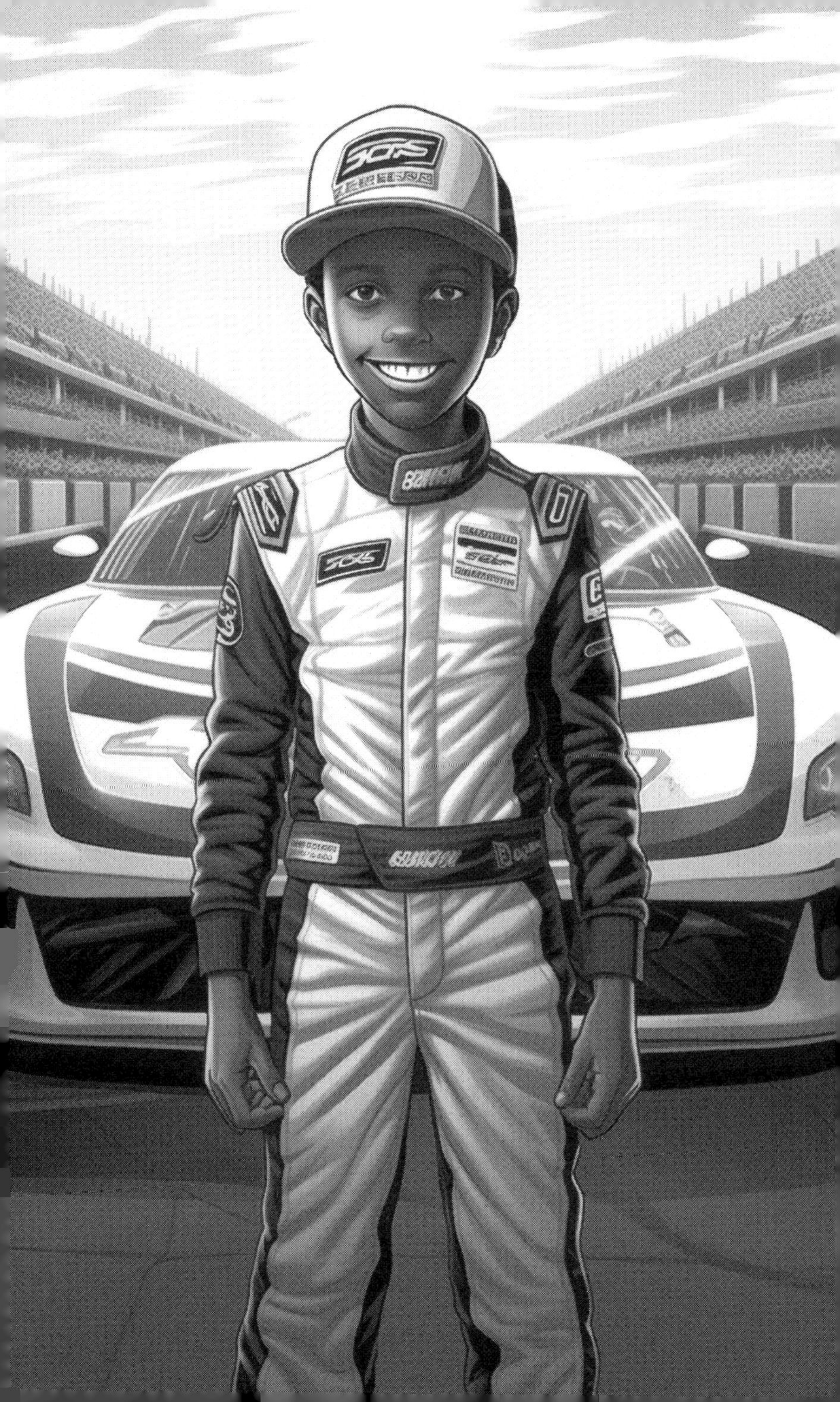

watching NASCAR races on television. He wondered what it would be like to drive one of those fast cars.

For Rajah's 12th birthday, his parents gave him an amazing birthday present. They took him to watch his first NASCAR race. Being at the race in person changed Rajah's life. From that moment on, he knew he wanted to drive race cars.

Rajah lived in the city though. There weren't big racetracks close by where Rajah could learn how to drive. Instead, he went online. He started doing a program called iRacing. Rajah had a lot to juggle! He was a good student, played basketball, ran track, and had a summer job. But he was determined to fit iRacing into his schedule, too.

iRacing was so cool! It was almost like driving a race car in real life. Rajah learned a lot and got better. Before too long, Rajah was selected to drive real race cars! Rajah got to be part of a program called NASCAR Drive for Diversity. Rajah is Black. There aren't many Black NASCAR drivers.

Rajah is happy to be living his childhood dreams. He gets to drive race cars fast around the tracks. He is racing cars and trucks. He has even won some races! Rajah feels like he is just getting started. At the heart of it all, is just a kid who has always loved cars and going fast.

4

Guy Fieri

Guy Fieri grew up in a family that loved to eat healthy foods. The problem was that sometimes the food seemed kind of bland and boring. Guy loved flavors and spice! He wanted to learn how to cook foods that had some pizazz.

When Guy was 10 years old, he went with his family on vacation. There he saw a food cart that sold soft pretzels. The

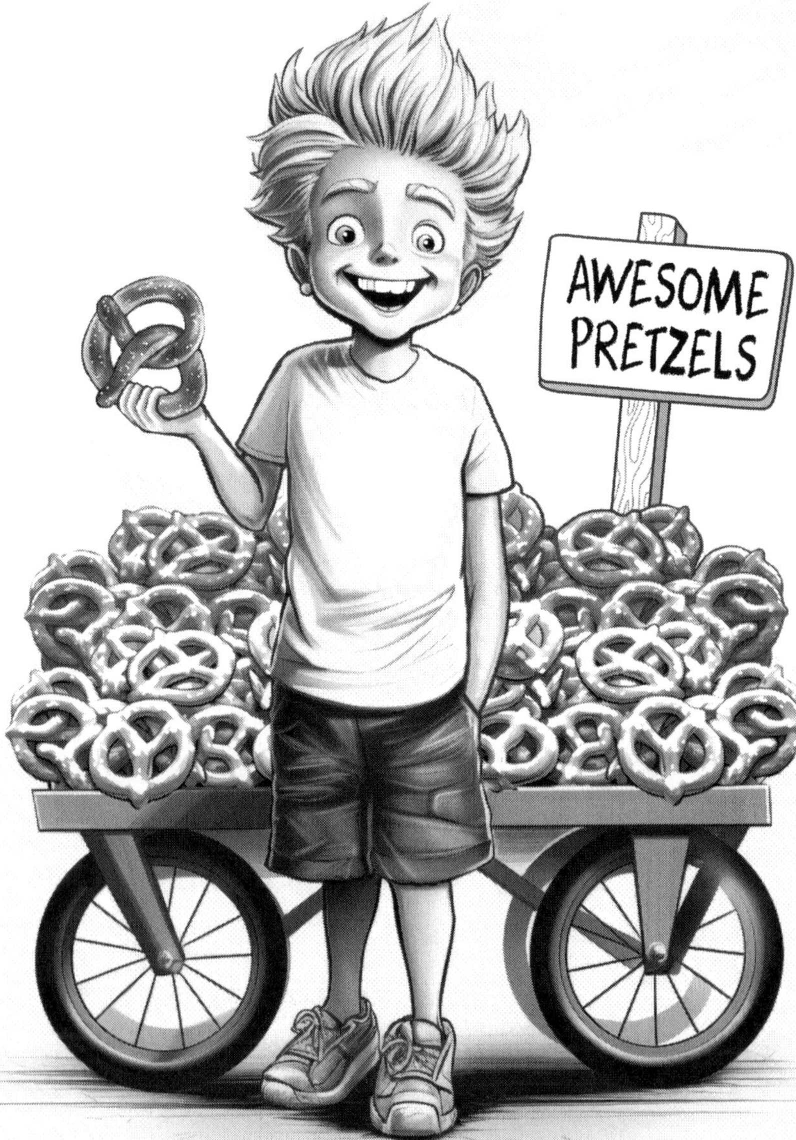
AWESOME
PRETZELS

pretzels were served hot, dipped
in thick salt, and drizzled
with mustard. Yum! Guy was
hooked. All of the flavors he
loved came shining through in
this delicious snack. Guy spent
all of his allowance on pretzels
that vacation. He came home
still dreaming about them.

Guy was a clever kid. He
knew that other kids in his
neighborhood would also love
the soft pretzels. He learned how
to make them. He and his dad
built a pretzel cart attached to
a three-wheeled bicycle. Guy
called his pretzel cart "Awesome
Pretzels". He pedaled all over the

neighborhood selling his yummy treat.

Guy saved up the money he earned. He also worked hard washing dishes to make money. Guy had big dreams. He knew he would need to earn and save money to make them work.

Guy wanted to travel. He wanted to learn more about food. Guy thought that the best place to do both of these things was France. When Guy was 16 years old, he became an exchange student. That means that he went to be a student in another country. Guy loved France. He loved the cozy diners and the little fruit and vegetable markets. He stayed in France for a year. He took a cooking class. Guy knew that he wanted to be a 'food guy' for the rest of his life!

When he came back home, Guy got to work. I think you understand that Guy worked really hard to make his dreams come true. Most people who have success work really hard. Guy went to college. He learned how to manage a restaurant. He worked in restaurants. He cooked food. Guy was all about his next big dream… Guy wanted to have his OWN restaurant.

Guy met some friends that helped him. The very first restaurant he opened was called Johnny Garlic's. The first restaurant was so popular that Guy was able to open other Johnny Garlic's in other cities.

Guy heard about a fun opportunity. The Food Network was a television channel all about cooking and food. The network hosted a reality show for chefs. The winner got to have their own cooking show series. Guy thought this seemed like the ultimate challenge. He entered the show and WON! Guy hosted his own show for the Food Network. *Guy's Big Bite* was on television for ten years. The Food Network liked Guy so much that they offered him another show. *Diners, Drive-Ins and Dives* is a show that lets Guy do all the things he loves. He gets to travel. He gets to visit cool restaurants, and he gets to eat yummy foods. Guy likes to talk to other restaurant owners. He likes to help people find cool new restaurants to try. He likes to try out new yummy food, just like all those years ago when he ate a soft pretzel for the very first time. Food and travel are some of Guy's favorite things. How cool that he gets to do them both?

With hard work and planning, Guy gets to spend his life doing things he loves to do. Do you have a dream that you are working hard to achieve? What do you need to learn or do to make that dream happen?

5

José Hernández

Have you ever failed at something and had to try again? How many times would you fail before you just gave up?

José Hernández doesn't know that answer because he never gave up. José applied to be an astronaut ELEVEN times. He was rejected ELEVEN times. He decided to try again. Finally, on his twelfth time, José got good

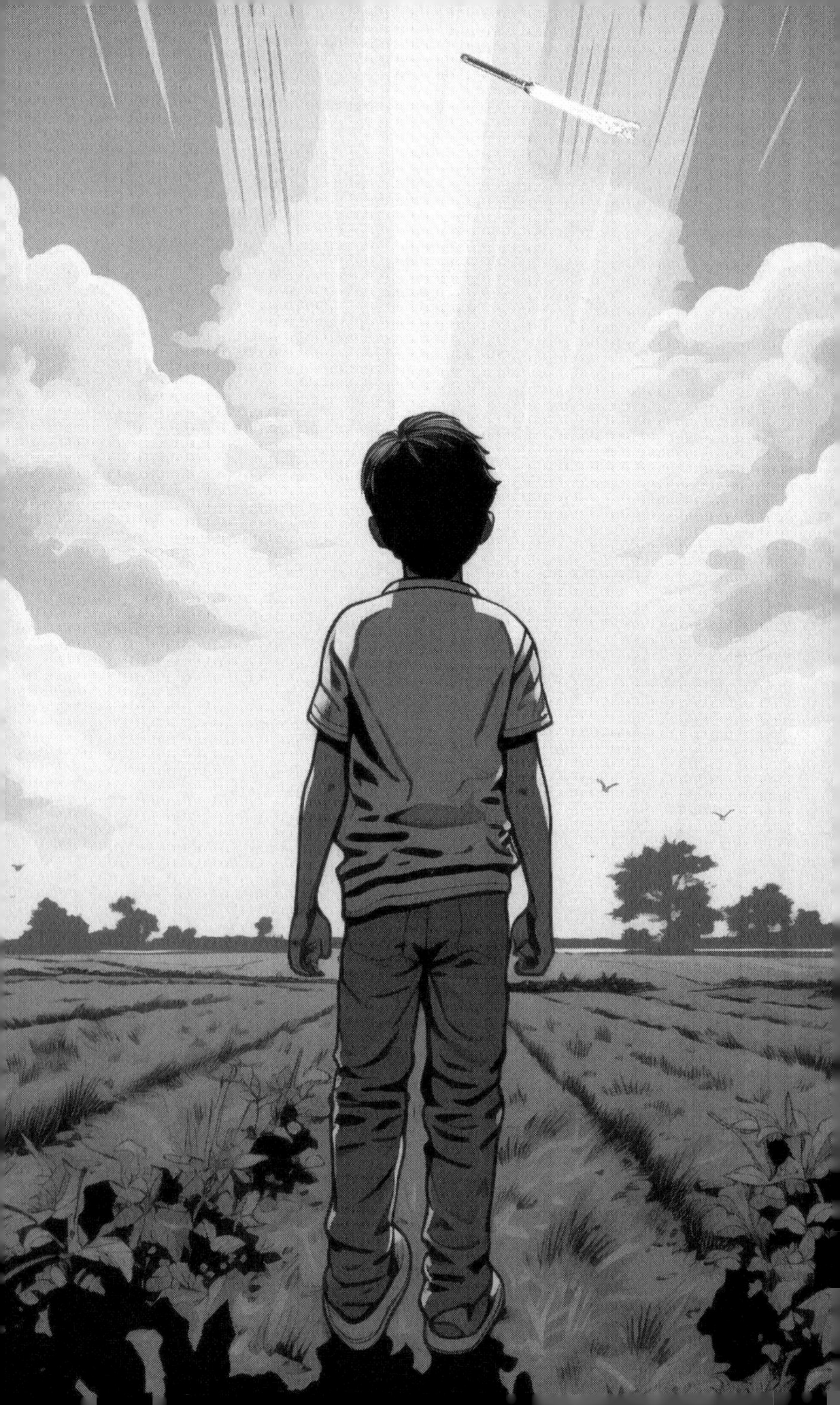

news. He was going to be an astronaut!

José grew up in Mexico and California. His parents were farm workers, and José and his family would travel to different farms. They would help grow and pick the crops. It was hard work. José often missed school if they were too busy working at a farm. Even though he was living in America, José did not learn to speak English until he was twelve years old.

One night, José was watching TV. He was ten. He saw an astronaut walking on the moon. "Wow!" José thought, "That's what I want to be."

José's family was poor. José didn't always go to school. He didn't speak English. How could he make his dreams happen?

José's father helped him along the way. He gave him a recipe for success. José applied this recipe to all of his dreams. This is José's recipe.

1. Determine your goal.
2. Recognize how far you are from it.
3. Draw yourself a roadmap.
4. Prepare for the challenge.
5. Work hard!

José got busy. He worked hard in school. He learned new things and met new people. When he sent in his astronaut application, he didn't give up. Even when he was rejected, José kept working for his dream.

When José was finally an astronaut, he got to spend 14 days up in space. He said the earth was so beautiful from out there.

Working toward a dream or goal is not always easy. It is important to work hard and stay focused. Even when things are challenging, it is important not to give up. You can use José's recipe to help you reach your goals, too.

6

Jimmy Donaldson

Have you ever heard of Jimmy Donaldson? What if I asked if you've ever heard of MrBeast? You might have heard of him! People love watching the MrBeast YouTube channel.

Jimmy started making videos when he was only 13 years old. Now his YouTube channel is seen by millions. That means Jimmy makes a lot of money doing what he loves.

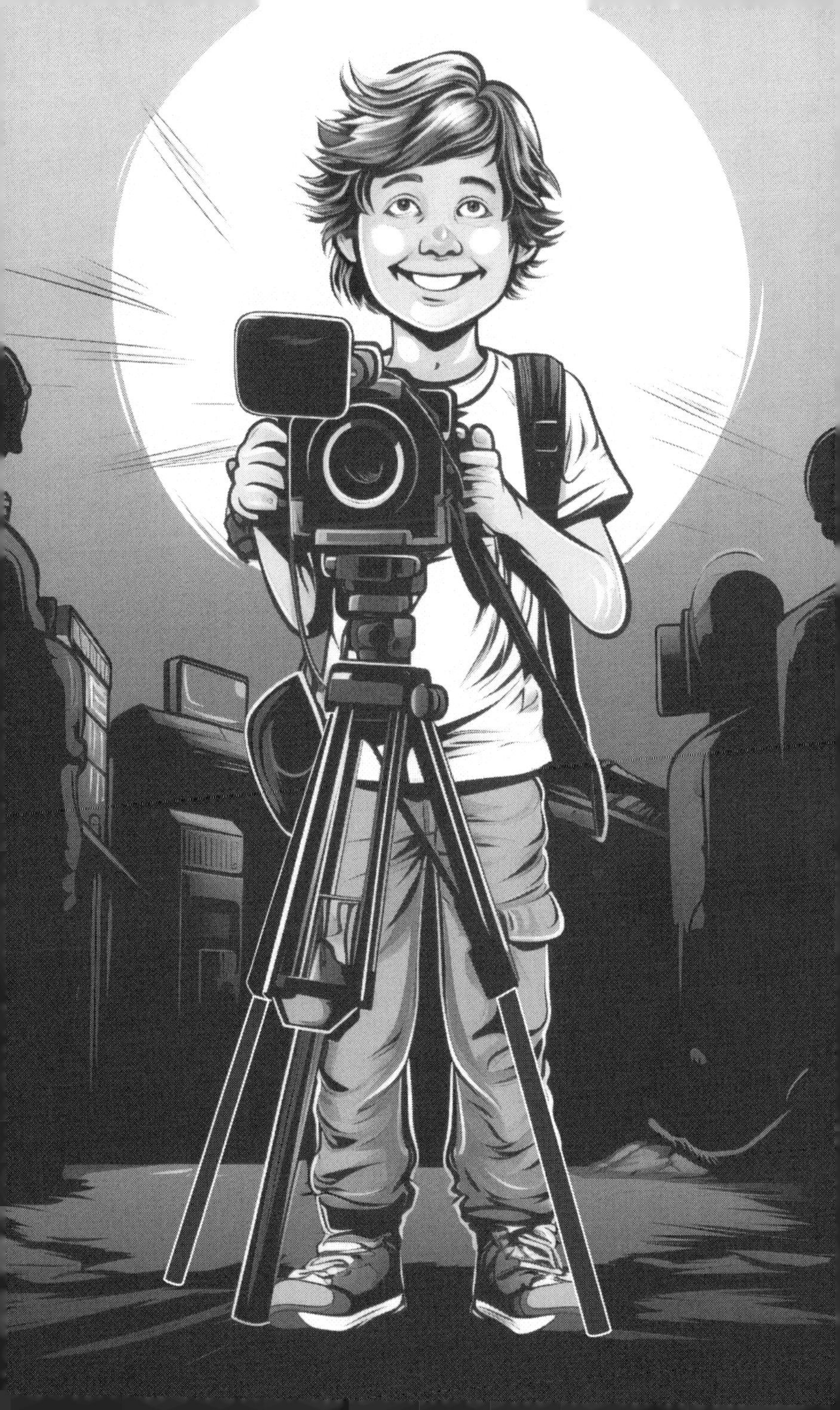

People didn't always watch the MrBeast YouTube channel. It took Jimmy a long time to gain followers. Jimmy was always excited about making fun videos. He had an old laptop computer and would film himself playing games. Then he would upload the videos to his YouTube channel. When he was just starting out, Jimmy didn't get many people to watch his videos. Still, he stuck with it. He liked making the videos. It's important not to give up easily. Especially if it is something that is important to you.

For five years Jimmy kept making videos, but they were

never very popular. Jimmy even quit college to focus on making more videos. He really wanted this to work. Finally, after five years, Jimmy made a video that went viral. That means lots of people saw the video and liked it. For that video, Jimmy counted from one to 100,000. Wow! I'll bet that took a long time. It did. It took Jimmy 40 hours to make that video! That actually sounds like a super boring video to watch, but it got lots of attention.

The MrBeast channel got more popular after that. Jimmy figured out that people wanted to watch new and crazy things. People liked watching interesting challenges. As his YouTube channel became more popular, Jimmy started making more money. He was smart about his money. Jimmy spent his money on his favorite thing. Making more videos! With the money he was making, Jimmy could make more videos. He could make them more exciting and interesting.

With his videos so interesting, more people started watching the MrBeast YouTube channel. Jimmy loved doing crazy challenges. He gives away a lot of money to people in the videos. He also likes to give away money to help people. Jimmy donated the money for 1,000 blind people to have surgery so they could see again. He started a challenge on Arbor Day. He wanted to raise 20 million dollars to plant trees. Jimmy used his YouTube channel to ask others to help him with his goal. So far, he has gotten more than 24 million trees planted in National Parks.

Jimmy is just getting going. He likes being creative and trying new things. He likes to come up with ideas that people haven't seen before. He likes to make videos that are exciting and he likes to help people along the way. The millions of followers of MrBeast are glad Jimmy didn't give up when his videos didn't make it right away. They are glad that Jimmy kept going and kept trying. What is something that is hard for you? Don't give up! You never know what can happen if you just keep trying!

7

George Washington Carver

Do you like peanut butter? If you do, you can thank George Washington Carver! George came up with the idea of peanut butter. In fact, he came up with 300 different ways that people could use the peanut.

George was an agricultural scientist. That means that George studied plants and the soil that helped them grow.

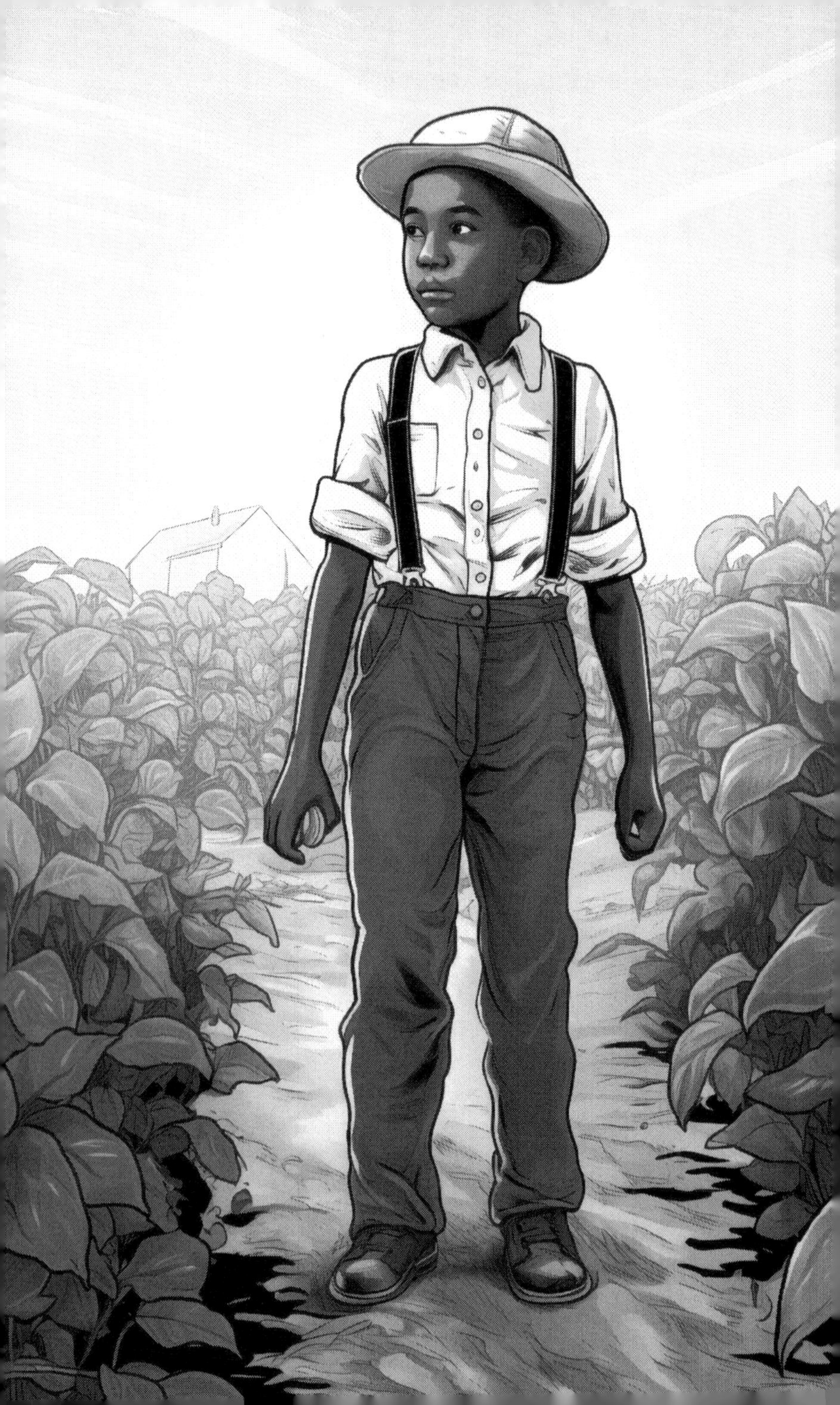

George loved plants. He loved working with farmers to teach them how to grow better crops.

When George was just a baby, his mom was a slave on a farm. George, his mom, and his sister were all kidnapped by some bad men. The owner of the farm tried hard to find them. He could only find George. The owners of the farm raised George and his brother as their own. They taught the boys how to read and write.

George's brother liked to go out in the fields and work on the farm with their foster dad. George was often sick as a child. He would stay at the house with his foster mom. She taught him to cook and work in the garden. He learned how to use plants to make simple medicines. George enjoyed working in the gardens and helping plants grow. He soon became known as "the plant doctor" to the local farmers. George was skilled at helping the farmers produce more crops.

Even though George liked plants and farming, he didn't want to live on that farm forever. George wanted to go to school to learn more. George graduated high school and went to college to study agriculture.

George got offered a job at an agriculture college in Alabama. He worked there for the rest of his life. When George first arrived, he said he needed two dorm rooms. One dorm for George to live in and one for his plants! George didn't really love the teaching part of the job. The students loved him, but George liked to stay busy out working the college farm. He liked working with local farmers. George still liked to help local farmers produce better crops.

George did research and studied. He knew the soil well. He told the farmers that they had to rotate their crops to make the soil better. This meant growing different types of crops in the soil each season. This would produce more crops each year. They would rotate the cotton crop with peanuts and sweet potatoes. But what would the farmers do with all these extra sweet potatoes and peanuts? No problem! George came up with many different ways to use these extra crops. He made a list of over 300 uses for peanuts. That's a lot!

George even came up with a way to help educate local farmers. He would travel in his Jessup wagon. He would travel to local farms and test their soil. He would give them advice on the best crops to grow. He would help make their farms better. George worked hard. He had a strong desire to help other people. He was a kind, caring man.

George loved helping plants and helping people. Many of his ideas, like crop rotation, are still used today. And nearly everyone loves peanut butter!

8

Matt Turner

Matt Turner is the United States men's soccer national team goalie. That's a really big deal and a very important position. What if I told you that he didn't even play soccer until he was in high school?

Matt grew up loving baseball. He decided to play soccer in high school. He thought playing soccer would help him stay in shape for baseball season. It

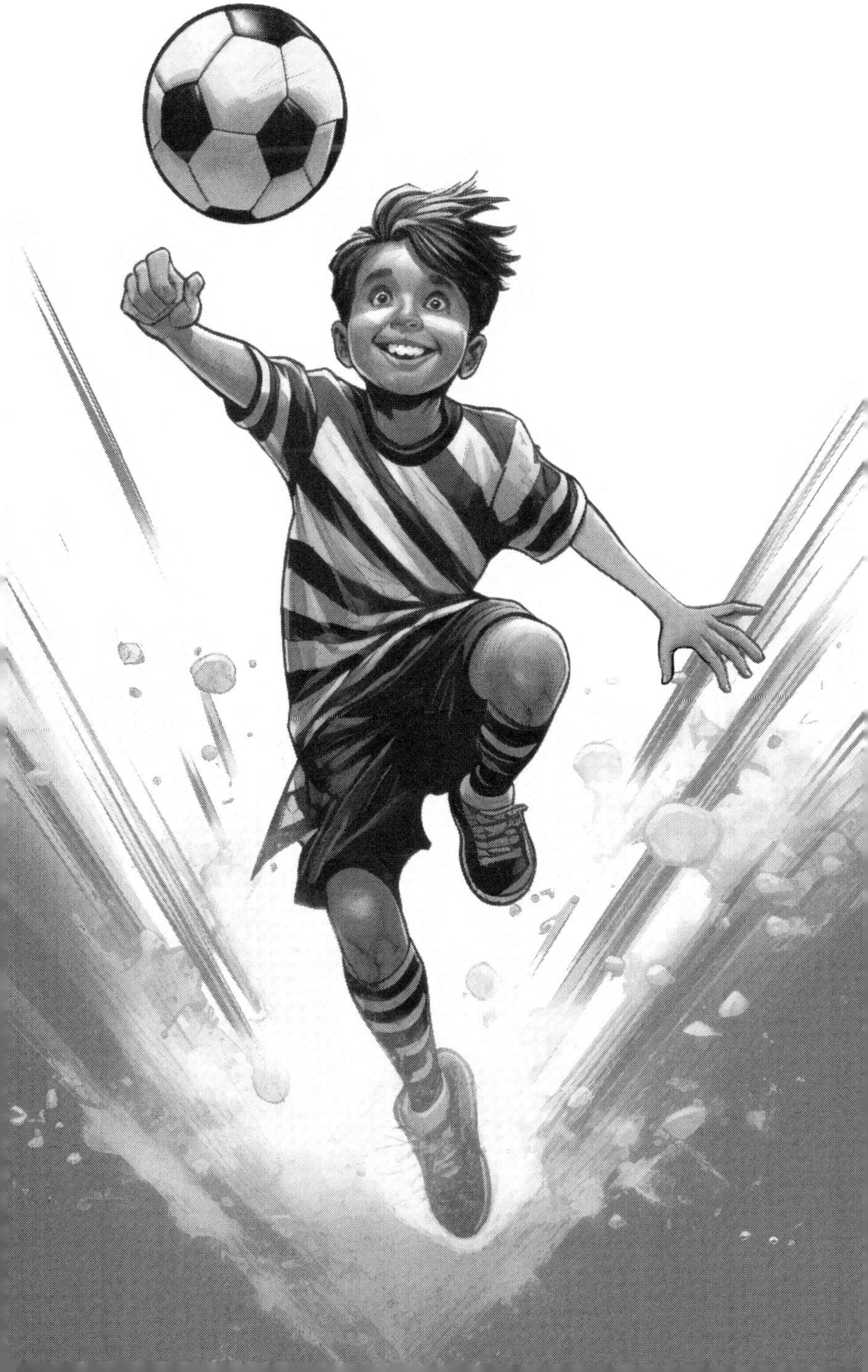

turned out that Matt was pretty good at soccer. He decided to try being a goalie. Matt had never played goalie before, but he wasn't afraid to try new things.

Matt worked hard. He was a pretty good goalie, but he was still new. After all, he'd only just started playing. Matt spent hours at the gym. He practiced until they turned off the lights. He worked hard at training camps all summer.

When Matt was in college, he played soccer, too. He finally got his chance to play in a big game. Matt was feeling good. He was really excited. He had worked so hard. Then something horrible happened. The other team kicked the ball. It hit the top crossbar and sailed straight up into the air. It came crashing back down. It went right in between Matt's arms. He missed an easy ball. It counted as a goal, and the other team won the game.

The video from that awful day went viral. It was played on television over and over again. Matt felt like a failure. Have you ever made a mistake? It can feel really bad to make a mistake. It's even worse when people tease you about it. Matt got teased. He thought about giving up soccer. "Maybe I should just quit," he thought.

What would you do if you were Matt? Matt loved soccer. He decided to keep playing. He decided to work hard and keep trying. It's important not to quit if something is important to you.

Just five years after that terrible day, Matt was the starting goalie for a professional soccer team. He's even won the "Goalkeeper of the Year" award twice. Matt now plays Premier League soccer and has played for his country (the USA) in a World Cup, the highest level of soccer in the entire world. It's a good thing Matt didn't quit when he had that bad game! Matt's story shows us that it's important to keep practicing, even on days when it's hard.

9

Neil deGrasse Tyson

Neil deGrasse Tyson had a lot of interests when he was growing up. He was a wrestler and wrote for his school's science magazine. He also did rowing and was a great dancer. When he was just 9 years old, Neil got to go to the planetarium. A planetarium is a big room with the ceiling lit up like the night sky. Neil thought

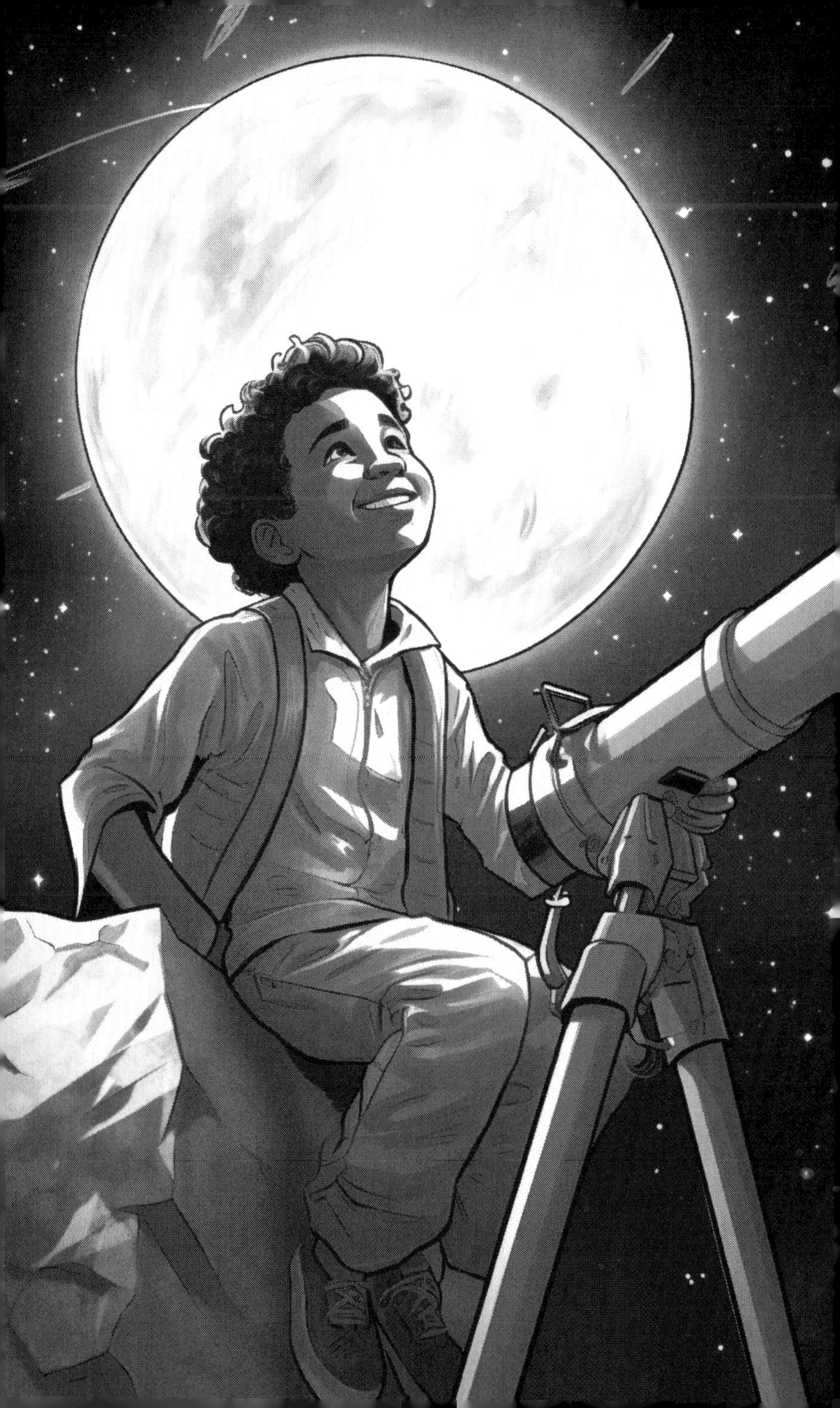

it was so cool! Neil felt like the universe was calling him. He became obsessed with stars. He wanted to learn more.

As a teenager, Neil spent a lot of time at that planetarium. He took astronomy classes. That's the study of stars and the universe. One of Neil's teachers was a really nice guy. He loved stars, too. He taught the class about stars in a way that was funny and exciting. Neil wanted to be like that. Neil decided he wanted to share his love of stars. He wanted to help people understand in ways that were fun and interesting.

Neil worked really hard. He studied and asked questions. Even as a young teenager, Neil was taking classes with really smart scientists. When he was just 15 years old, Neil got to teach a class about stars. That's really young to be the teacher!

Neil went to college to study astronomy. He studied and did research. Neil worked hard. He helped scientists learn new things about the universe. He made being a scientist very cool.

Neil got the chance to be the director of the first planetarium that inspired him all those years ago. Neil remembered all the teachers and scientists who helped him learn about stars. It meant a lot to him that now he would get to help people, too.

Neil really likes to help other people learn about the stars and the universe. He has written books and taught classes. Neil has been on television lots of times. He even has his own show called *StarTalk*. Neil remembers the funny teacher from when he was young.
Neil also likes to teach people by keeping things fun and exciting. Thanks to Neil's fun approach, both kids and adults love learning more about the universe.

10

Henry Ford

Do you like to tinker with things? Do you take your toys apart and try to put them back together? When Henry Ford was a boy, he did the same thing. Yes, the inventor of the first automobile was always taking things apart and putting them back together.

Henry Ford was born on a farm in Michigan. He attended a one-room school with his

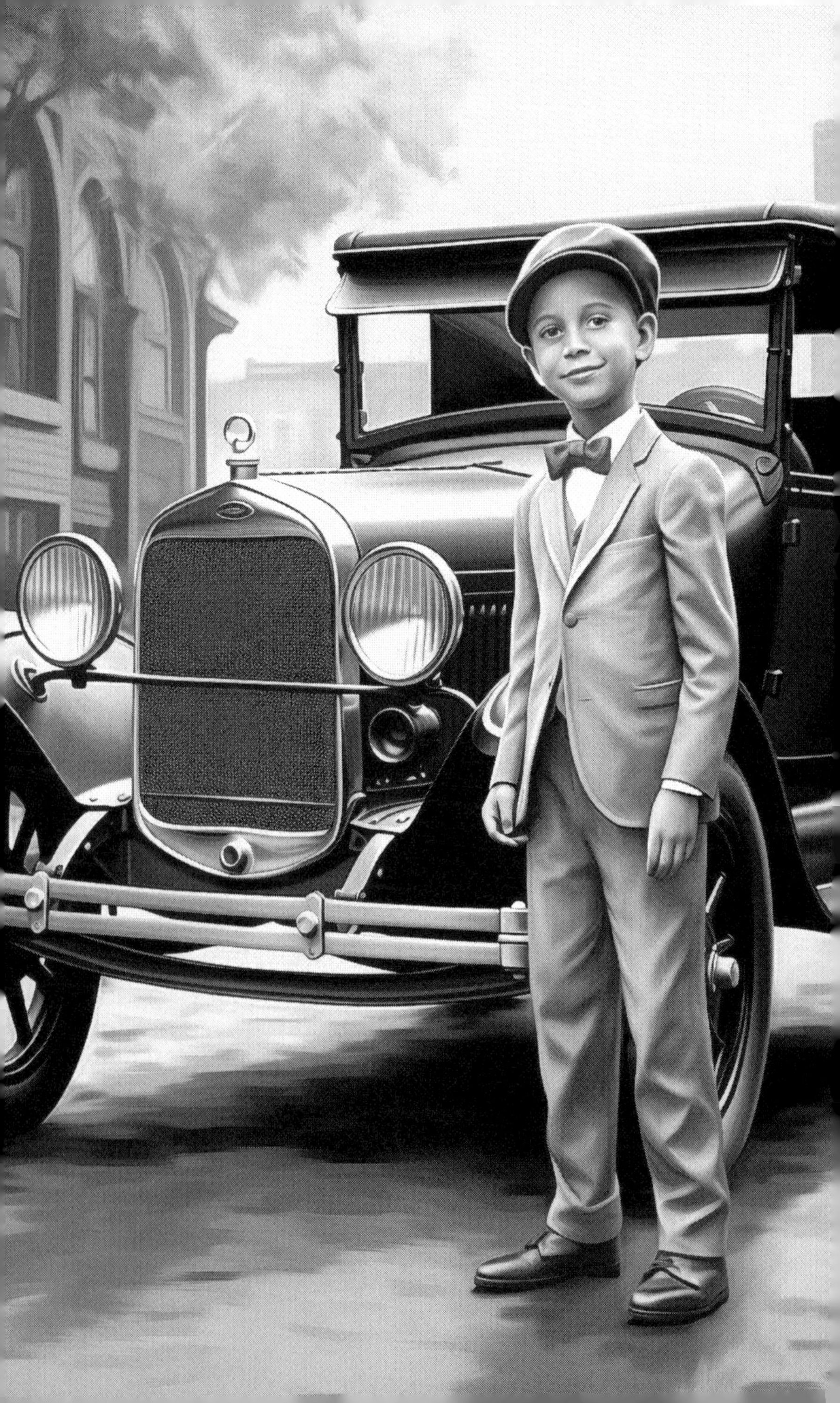

younger brothers and sisters. Henry didn't really like school very much. He didn't like to read or write. His favorite thing to do was tinker. When he was 12 years old, Henry was given a watch. He took that watch apart and put it back together many times. He became an expert on watches. In his little town, Henry was asked to fix watches for many people. He understood how all the gears and parts worked.

Henry's father thought that Henry would grow up and run the farm, but Henry had other dreams. He loved seeing how machines worked. He went to learn about being an engineer. He learned how to operate small machines. He learned how to make repairs to steam engines.

Henry worked for years as a chief engineer. When he wasn't at work, Henry had a side project. He was trying to make a small engine that used gasoline and air to work. This was different from the big steam engines of the day.

Finally, Henry figured out the engine and produced his automobile. Other people were also trying to make automobiles. The problem was that the first cars were so expensive to make. Only the very, very rich could afford a car. Henry wanted to change this.

Henry went back to tinkering. He came up with the idea for an affordable car. He figured out how to make the car as cheaply as possible. Henry called his car the Model T. The first Model T sold for $850. This was way more affordable than other cars. The Model T didn't have any fancy parts. It only came in one color, black. Still, the demand for the Model T grew. Everyone wanted to have one.

Since more people wanted to have a Model T, Henry had to figure out how to make more cars fast! He came up with the idea for the assembly line. This made it easier for his workers to do their work. They could work faster and better. Henry knew that happy workers did the best work. He gave all of his workers raises. He doubled his workers' pay. He shortened the workers' day from nine hours to just eight hours. Henry also let his workers take both Saturday AND Sunday off from work. He actually invented the weekend!

Why did Henry do all of these things for his workers? Henry knew that if his workers were happy, rested, and well-paid, they would be motivated to do a good job. They would work fast. They would produce more cars. More cars made Henry more money. Henry was a wise businessman.

The Model T changed the world. Making cars affordable changed how people did everything. People could get from one place to another faster. Imagine if you didn't have a family car. You might have a horse and carriage instead. Would you like that? It would take you a lot longer to get places!

Henry Ford was an innovator. He liked solving problems. Even though he didn't really like school, Henry was very smart.

11

Jackie Robinson

Jackie Robinson is known as one of the greatest baseball players of all time. Jackie had 137 home runs in his career. He played in six World Series. He was voted as the National League's Most Valuable Player (MVP). All of those things are amazing. Perhaps the greatest thing that Jackie Robinson did was to help Black people and

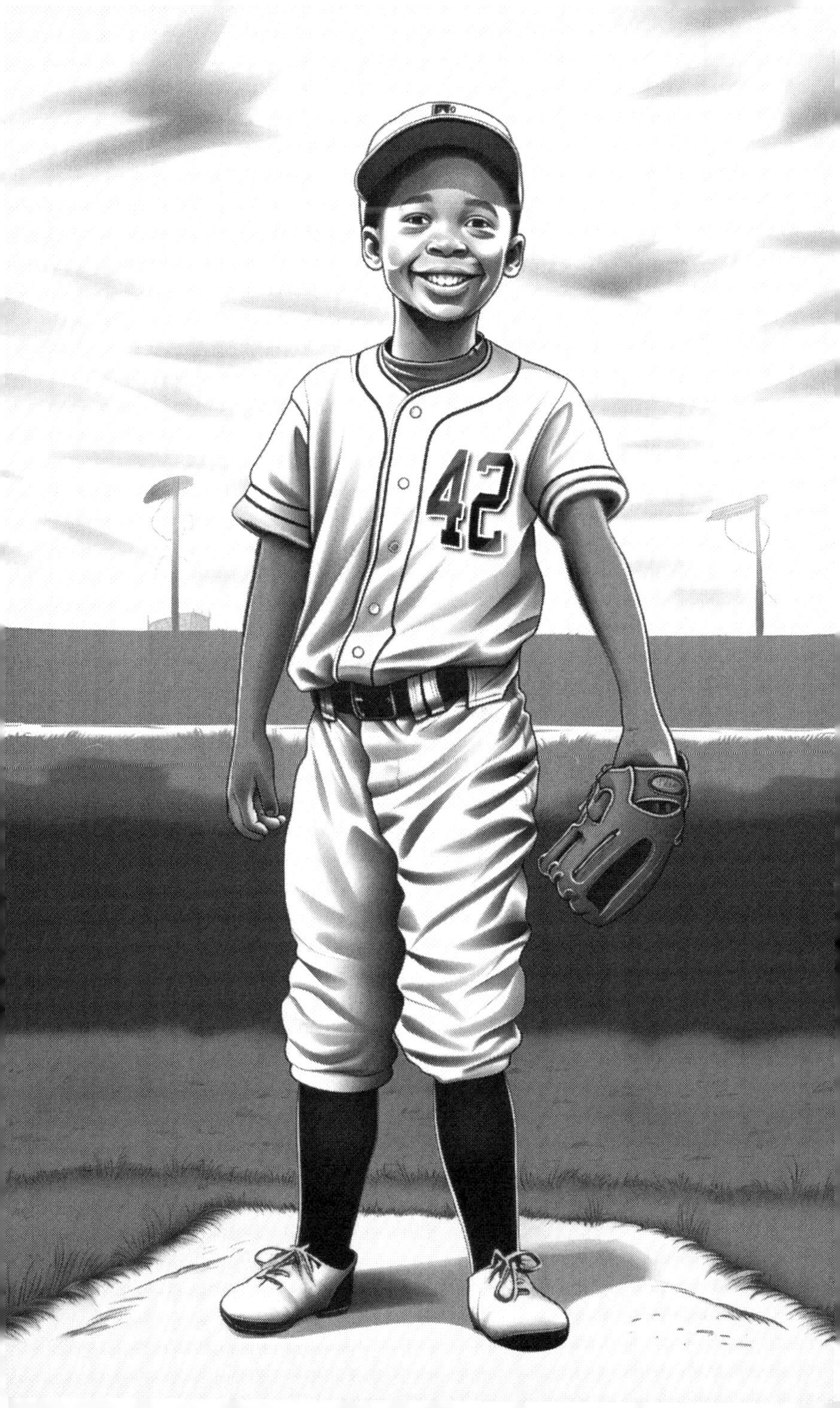
42

White people come together to play the game of baseball.

Jackie played baseball in the 1940s. Back then, Black people and White people did things separately. They ate at separate restaurants. They sat in different parts of the bus. They played on different sports teams. This is called segregation. Many people disagreed with segregation. It took people that were very brave to stand up and change the way that things were.

Jackie Robinson grew up in California with three brothers and sisters. He liked to play sports. Jackie played football, baseball, and basketball. He ran track and played tennis. In high school, Jackie was the quarterback of the football team and the star baseball player. But the kids at his school weren't always nice to him. Jackie was Black and he looked different than everybody else. Have you ever felt left out because of the way you look?

Jackie continued to be a star at sports all through college. People were starting to take note of what an amazing baseball player he was. He got asked to play professional baseball for a Black baseball team. Then, later that same year, Jackie was asked to make history.

Team managers wanted to find a way to get Black people and White people playing baseball together. They needed a really brave person to be the first ballplayer to do it. They also needed the best. The managers chose Jackie. He was an excellent baseball player. Most importantly, they knew he was brave.

It would be scary to be the first Black player. People weren't always nice. Sometimes even his own teammates didn't seem to like playing with a Black player. As the season went on, Jackie showed them what he was made of. He was tough, but he didn't fight back when people said mean things. He worked hard on playing baseball. He showed them how good he was on the field.

Jackie helped The Dodgers make it to the World Series. He was named Rookie of the Year. Jackie would go on to play in five more World Series. He played professional baseball for ten years. After Jackie started playing baseball, more teams began to integrate Black players onto their teams. Jackie opened the doors to Blacks and Whites playing baseball together.

It can be hard to feel different or left out. It is even harder when people say mean things or make you feel bad about the way you look or act. It is important to remember that you are special just the way you are.

12

Steve Irwin

What is the coolest birthday present you have ever received? When Steve Irwin turned six, he was given a twelve-foot-long python snake. Woah! I'm not sure if that is cool or creepy. Luckily, Steve thought it was cool. He named the snake Fred.

Steve was born in Australia. His parents were both wildlife experts. I guess that's how he got the snake. By the time

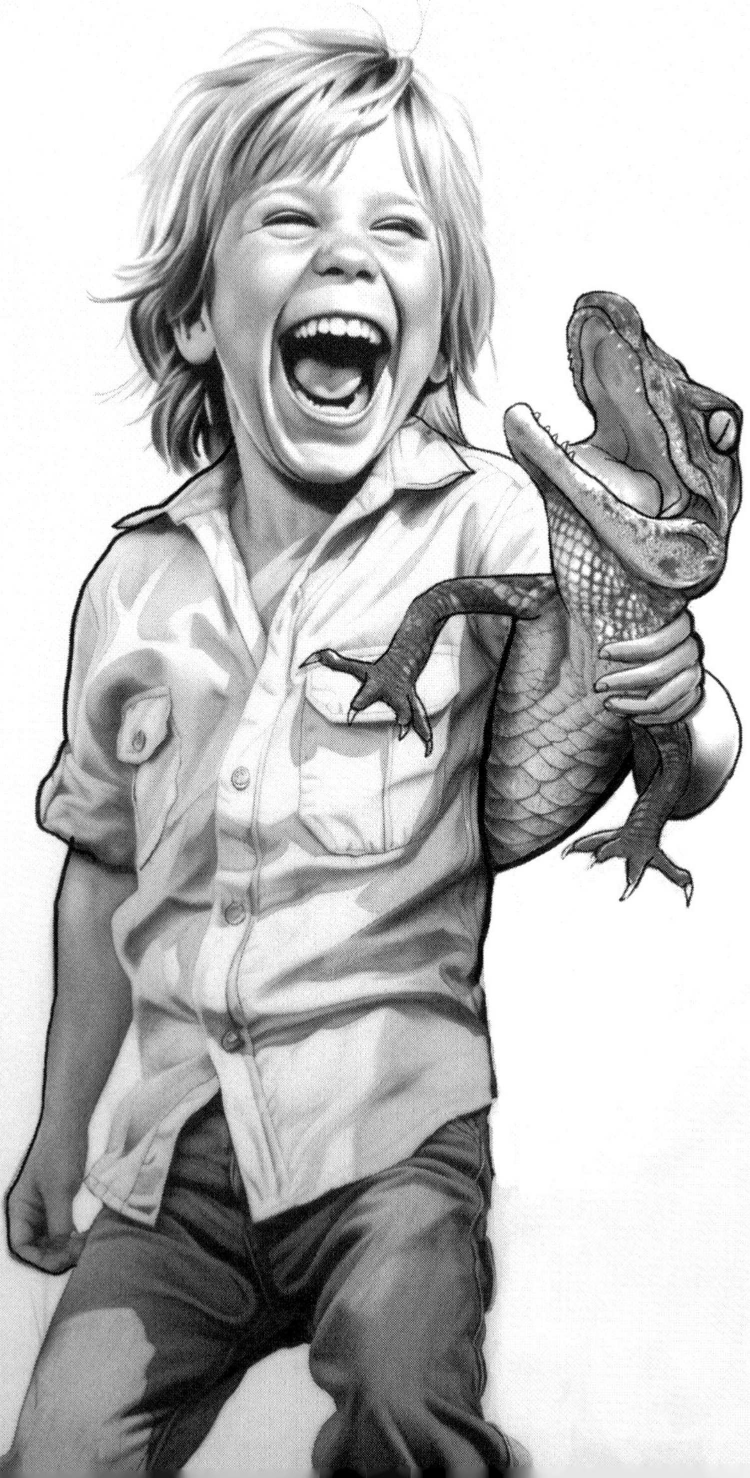

he was nine years old, Steve was helping his dad handle crocodiles. His parents owned a small reptile zoo. Steve worked at the zoo. He helped feed and take care of all the creatures living there.

Steve's favorite thing to do was catch crocodiles. Steve and his dad would get a call if a crocodile was seen in a busy area. They would go and wrestle the crocodile and catch it. Then they would take the crocodile to an area that was safe for both the crocodile and the humans. It was dangerous work, but Steve loved it!

Steve grew up and got married. His wife's name was Terri. She loved wildlife, too. Steve and Terri liked to teach people about animals. They wanted people to know about nature and the environment. They knew that if people learned more about the earth, they would take better care of it. It was important to Steve to take care of the earth and all the creatures living on it.

Steve was nice and funny. People liked him. Steve started filming a show about crocodiles. The show was called *Crocodile Hunter*. Many people watched the show and learned about crocodiles and protecting the earth. This made Steve happy. Steve was fun to watch. He would wrestle crocodiles, catch poisonous snakes, and play with lizards.

Do you love animals? Steve did, too. Steve called himself a wildlife warrior. He thought the most important work he could do was to help animals. He wanted to teach everybody that they could make a difference for our earth. Steve inspired a lot of people to take care of animals and the planet.

Steve died in an accident when he was stung by a stingray. His family continues to teach people about animals. Steve's love of animals and his message about protecting the earth are still alive today. Thanks to Steve sharing his love of animals, many people today take better care of the earth.

13

Alfred Nobel

You would think that the inventor of dynamite would be a wild guy who enjoyed fighting, right? Wrong! Alfred Nobel hated war. What he loved... was science. Let's learn a little more about this guy who left behind an important message.

Alfred Nobel was born into a poor family. His dad was a hard worker and very smart. He was good at business. He worked

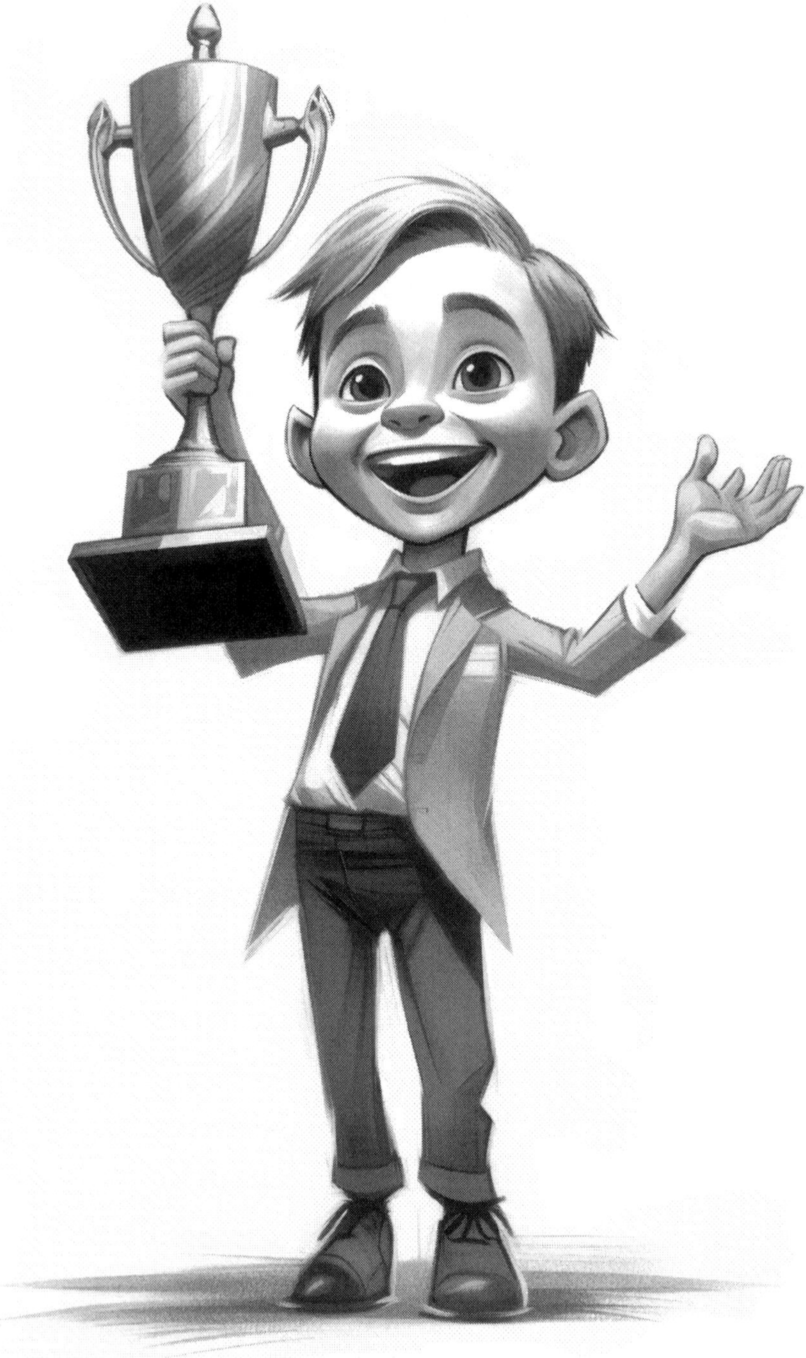

hard to give his family a better life. Alfred learned a lot from his dad.

Alfred liked to learn about science. Like a lot of boys, he liked making things explode. He studied ways to make things blow up. He met the guy who had discovered nitroglycerin. That is one of the key ingredients in dynamite. The other scientist warned him of the danger of nitroglycerin. It would sometimes blow up without warning. It was very dangerous.

Alfred thought he could learn more and maybe make nitroglycerin useful. He studied and worked hard. He wanted to make safe explosives.

Then a sad thing happened. Alfred's brother was working on a project using nitroglycerin. It exploded and Alfred's brother was killed. Alfred was so upset. He worked even harder to find a way to make a safe explosive. He invented dynamite because it made the nitroglycerin safe to use.

When Alfred's brother died, a crazy thing happened. The newspaper ran an article about the death. But they got mixed up! They said that Alfred had died in the explosion. The article talked about what a horrible invention dynamite was. The article said a lot of unkind things about Alfred. Many of them were untrue. But it made Alfred think.

Alfred didn't want to be remembered just as the inventor of dynamite. He wanted to leave behind something good in the world. He thought hard about it. He asked his friends. This was what he came up with.

Alfred had made a lot of money being a scientist. He decided that when he died, he would start a prize program. He would leave all his money to this prize program. Each year a group of judges picks five people who have helped humans the most in the last year. The prize categories are science, medicine, chemistry, literature, and peace. Alfred wanted to encourage people to do good things. He wanted to encourage people to study and make people's lives better.

The Nobel Prize is still a huge honor given out today. It is well known around the whole world. Alfred may have invented dynamite, but his goal of being remembered for something good came true. People think about peace when they think of Alfred's name. That's because the Nobel Peace Prize has his name right there on it. Most people today don't remember that he invented dynamite. Mission accomplished!

14

Dwayne Johnson

You might know Dwayne Johnson better by his wrestling name, The Rock. Dwayne was born into a family of wrestlers. His dad and his grandpa both wrestled. Even his grandma was really involved in wrestling! But Dwayne didn't dream of growing up and becoming a wrestler. That came later.

When he was growing up, Dwayne's family moved around

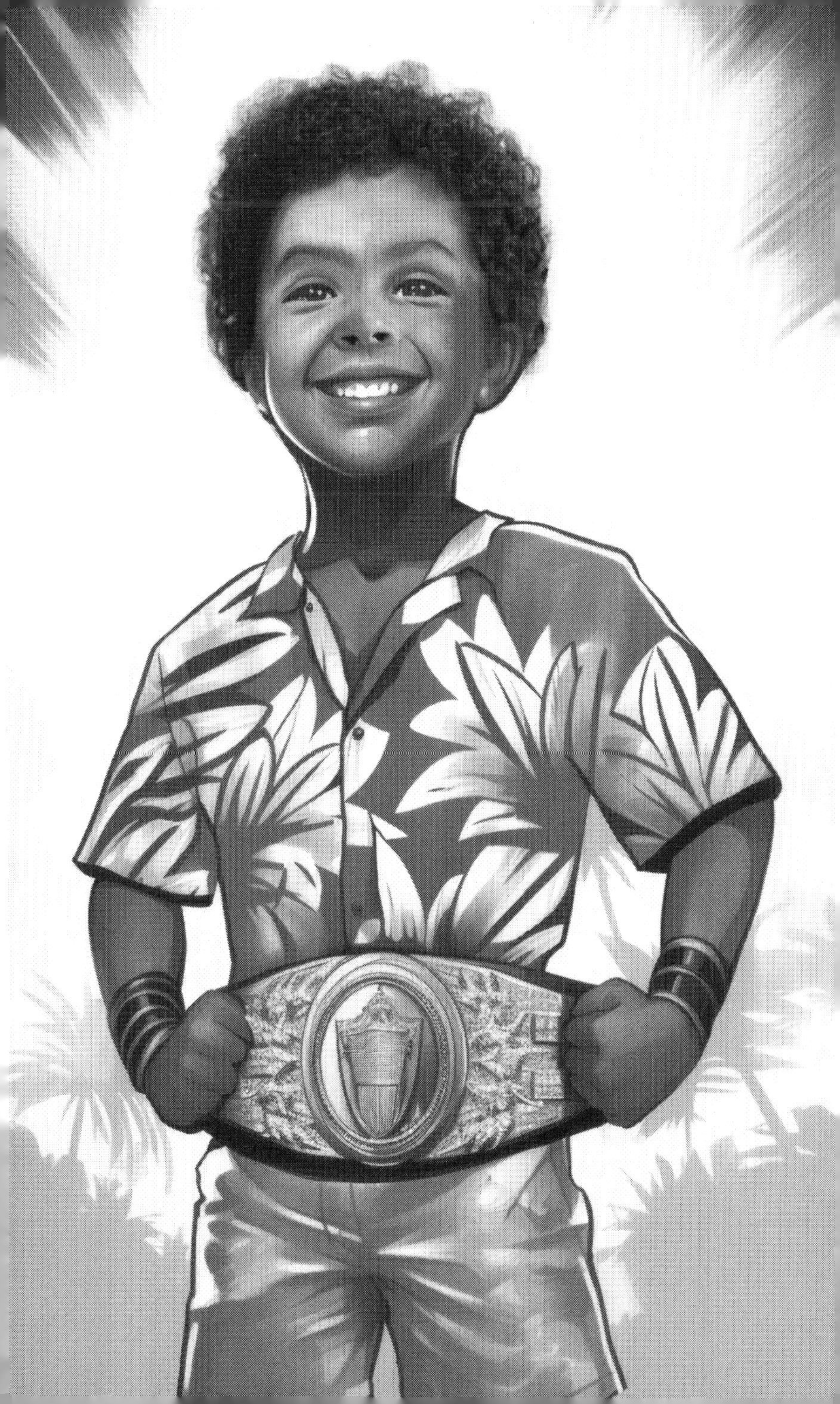

a lot. He had to go to new schools and meet lots of new kids. That was hard for Dwayne. Even as a kid, he was bigger than most other kids his age. Dwayne got picked on. He got made fun of. He had a hard time making friends. Dwayne started getting into fights. It seemed like he was always getting into trouble. Things were not going well for Dwayne. Have you ever acted out when things weren't going your way? Did you get in trouble? What helped you to get back on the right path?

Dwayne moved to another new school. One of the coaches at this school asked him to try out for the football team. Dwayne loved it! After that, Dwayne didn't get into trouble anymore. The coach encouraged him to do and act his best. Dwayne spent all his time and energy playing football. He worked hard to be a good player and teammate. It is important to have someone who encourages you to do your best.

Dwayne got to play football in college. Then he got injured. It was bad. He knew that he wouldn't get to be a professional football player. His dream was over. He was really sad for a little while. But he didn't stay sad for long. He knew that he needed a new dream.

It would have been easy to give up. But that's not who Dwayne was. He just changed his plan. Dwayne was an athlete. He liked to perform. He asked his dad to help him learn to wrestle. He was getting into the family business!

Dwayne was an excellent wrestler. He wrestled for the World Wrestling Federation and had fans all over the country. He became the most popular wrestler and won many championships. He became known as Dwayne "The Rock"

Johnson. He was just getting started.

Dwayne got asked to be in a movie. He really liked it and he did a good job. He got asked to be in more movies. He was a natural performer and people loved him. Soon, Dwayne was a Hollywood superstar!

Dwayne continued to wrestle for a long time. He has starred in many movies and even helps make them. Dwayne's story shows us that it is important to have someone believe in you. It is also important to set goals and have dreams. Even if you are getting into trouble, you can always change and make good choices. You just have to believe in yourself!

YOUR REVIEW

What if I told you that just one minute out of your life could bring joy and jubilation to everyone working at a kids book company?

What am I yapping about? I'm talking about leaving this book a review.

I promise you, we take them **VERY seriously**. Don't believe me?

Each time right after someone just like you leaves this book a review, a little siren goes off right here in our office. And when it does we all pump our fists with pure happiness.

A disco ball pops out of the ceiling, flashing lights come on... it's party time!

Roger, our marketing guy, always and I mean always, starts flossing like a crazy person and keeps it up for awhile. He's pretty good at it. (It's a silly dance he does, not cleaning his teeth)

Sarah, our office manager, runs outside and gives everyone up and down the street high fives. She's always out of breath when she comes back but it's worth it!

Our editors work up in the loft and when they hear the review siren, they all jump into the swirly slide and ride down into a giant pit of marshmallows where they roll around and make marshmallow angels. (It's a little weird, but tons of fun)

So reviews are a pretty big deal for us.

It means a lot and helps others just like you who also might enjoy this book, find it too.

You're the best!
From all of us goofballs at Big Dreams Kids Books